The Clumsy

Ballerina

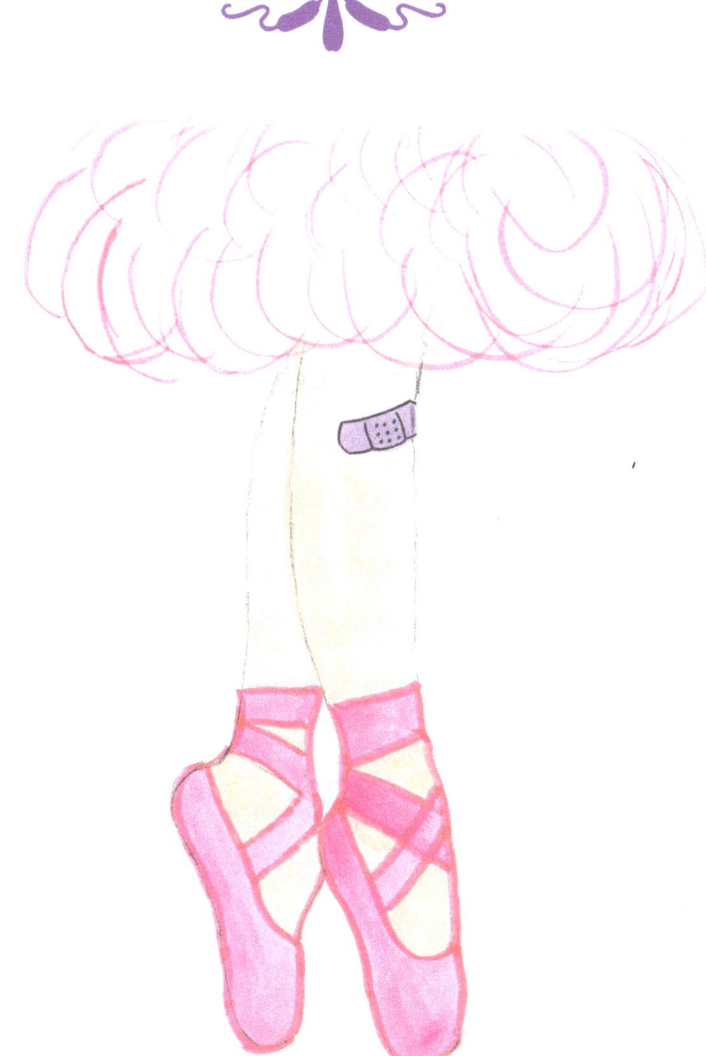

Sofia & Deanna Ghannam

Balboa Press books may be ordered through booksellers or by contacting:

Balboa Press
A Division of Hay House
1663 Liberty Drive
Bloomington, IN 47403
www.balboapress.com
1 (877) 407-4847

ISBN: 978-1-5043-4962-8 (sc)
ISBN: 978-1-5043-4963-5 (e)

Library of Congress Control Number: 2016901005

Print information available on the last page.

Balboa Press rev. date: 2/19/2016

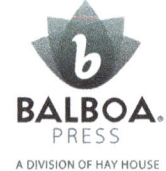

BALBOA
PRESS

A DIVISION OF HAY HOUSE

Dance is the hidden language of the soul of the body

– Martha Graham

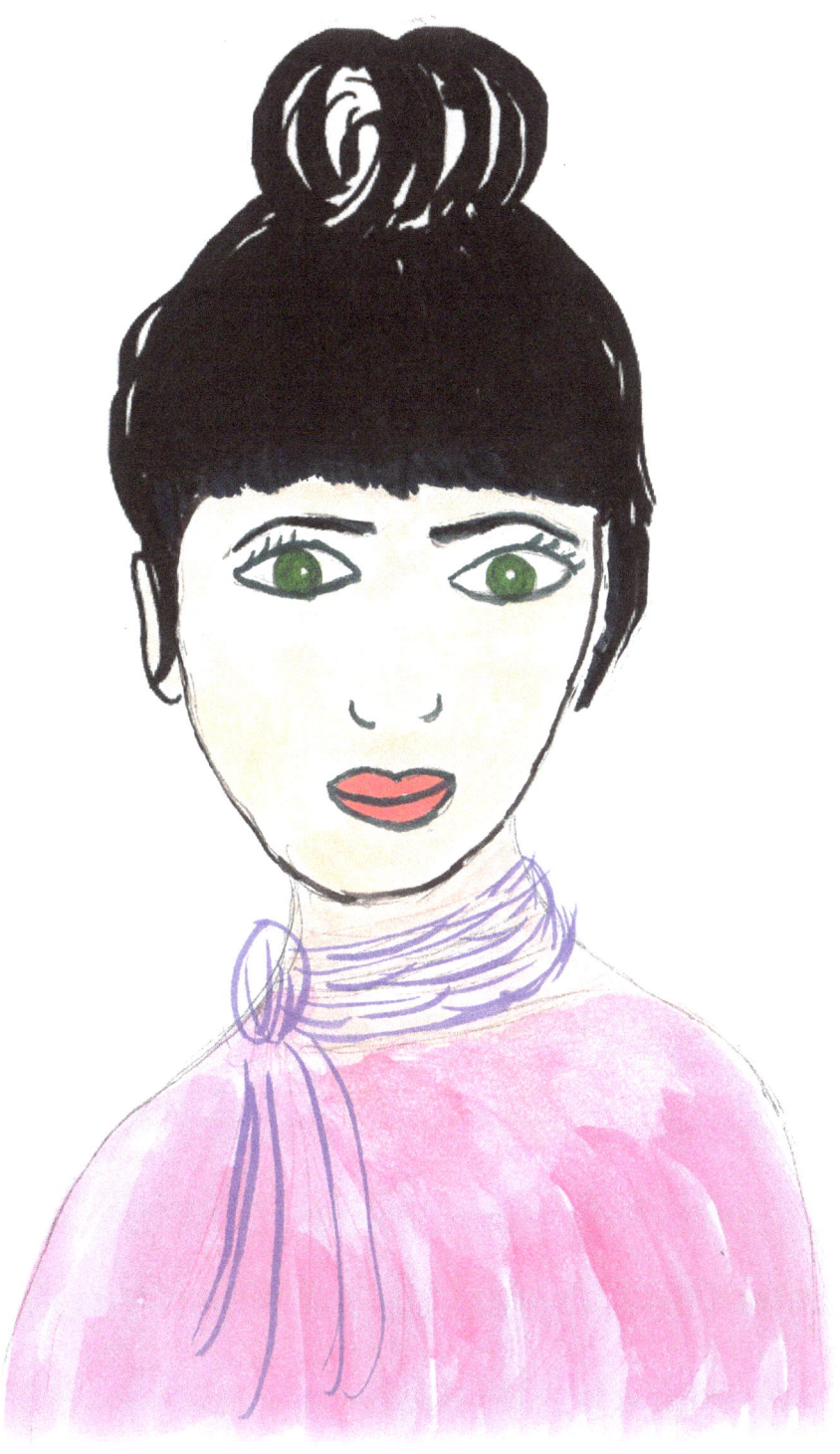

"One - two - three" yells Ms. Anaïs, "Plié, point your toes Scarlett! Battement frappé Scarlett, not battement tendu! Your feet are wrong! How many times do I have to tell you! Learn from your sister Siena, her feet are perfect! She dances like an angel"...

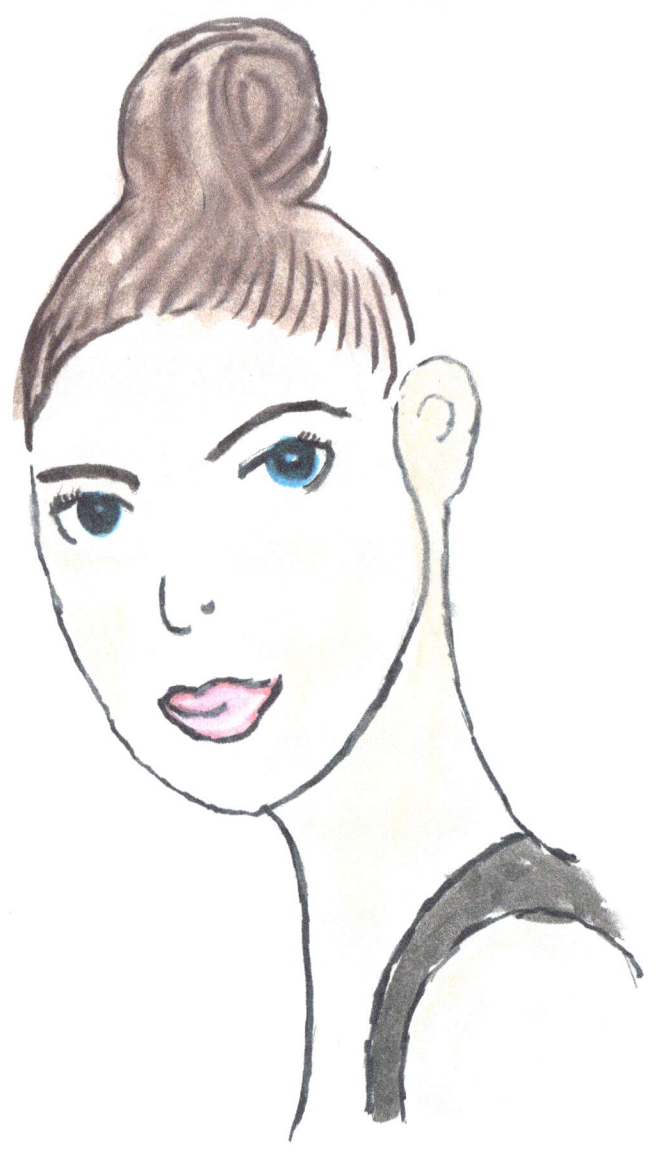

My twin sister Siena always gets the praise from the teacher. I am always in the back, and I never get picked for the good roles. I'm happy for Siena. She is a very good dancer, and I don't want to get jealous because she is my twin sister, but I wish I would get noticed sometimes. "We have been taking ballet since we were 3 years old. We are 11 now. Maybe I wasn't meant to be a ballerina." Scarlett says to Siena.

"Don't say that Scarlett, you are a great dancer, you just need more training." Siena explains to Scarlett, "I don't want you to give up."

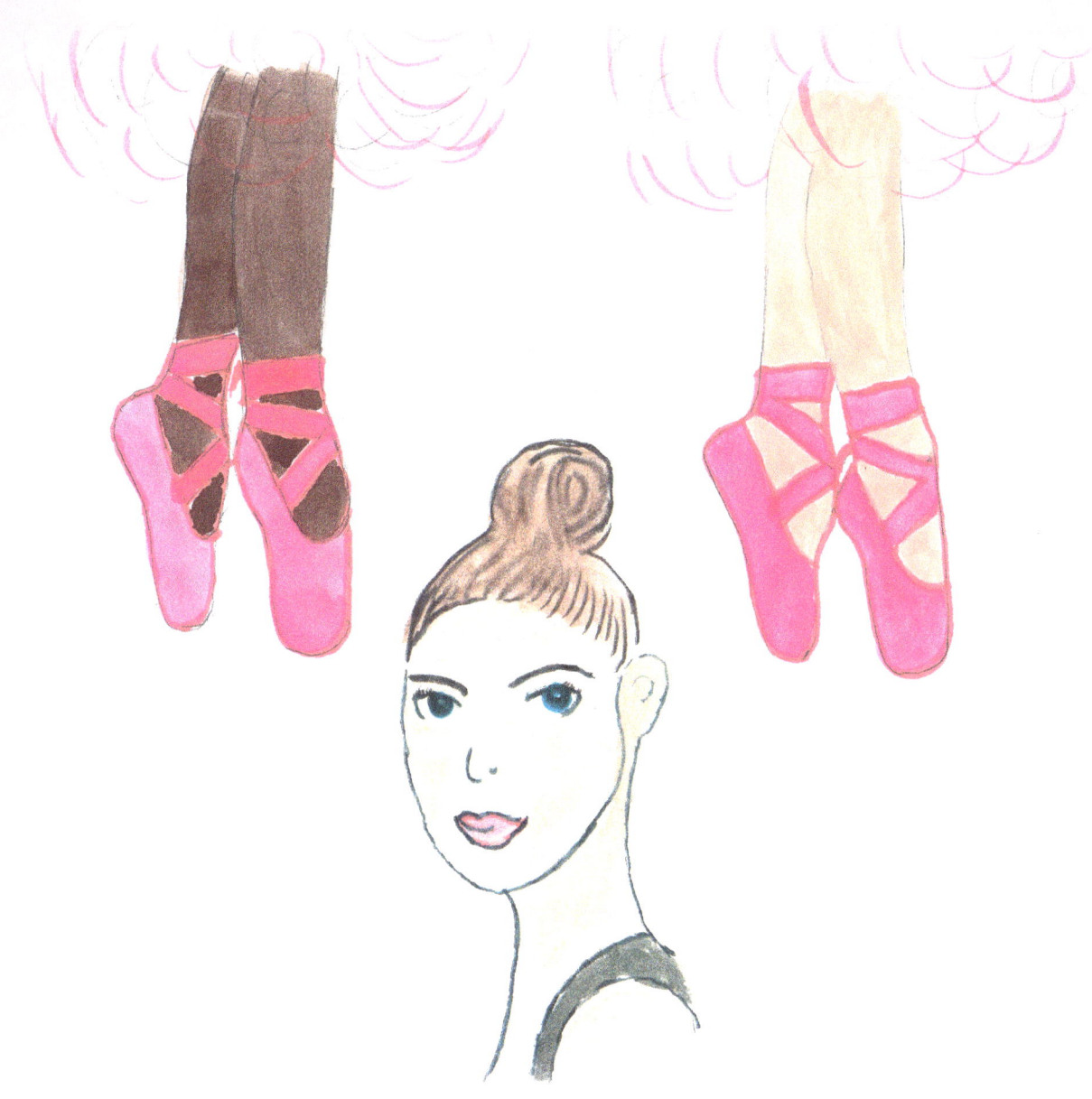

"Today we are going to start rehearsing for the recital. I wanted to pick the dancer that has improved so much this year. This dancer is such an asset to our dance studio; she will be performing the main solo this year." Ms. Anaïs says to her students, "The dancer this year is Siena. The background dancers will be Jennifer, Anna, Madeline, & Scarlett. I choreographed it myself; the title of the dance is "Le Petit Fleur". Don't screw it up Scarlett!"

"Whoopee, I'm in the background again." Scarlett sarcastically thinks to herself.

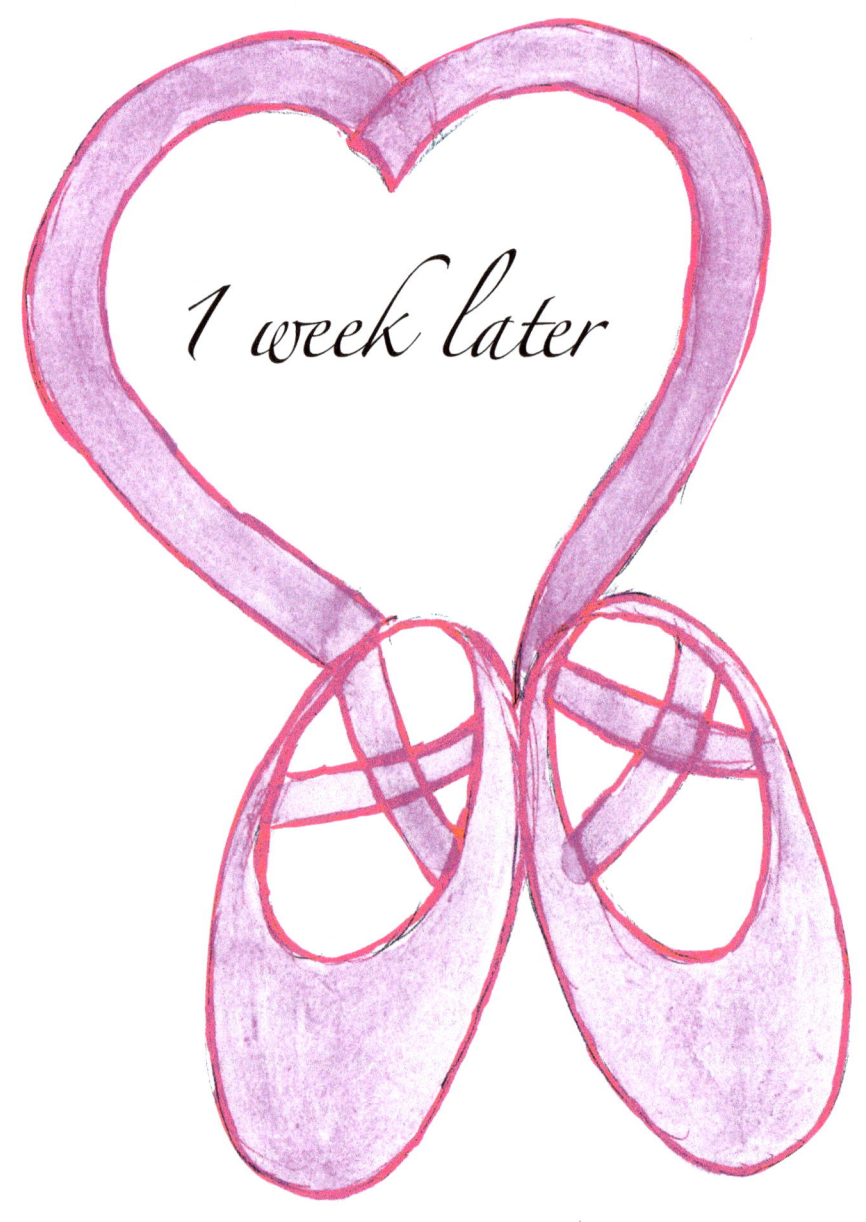

1 week later

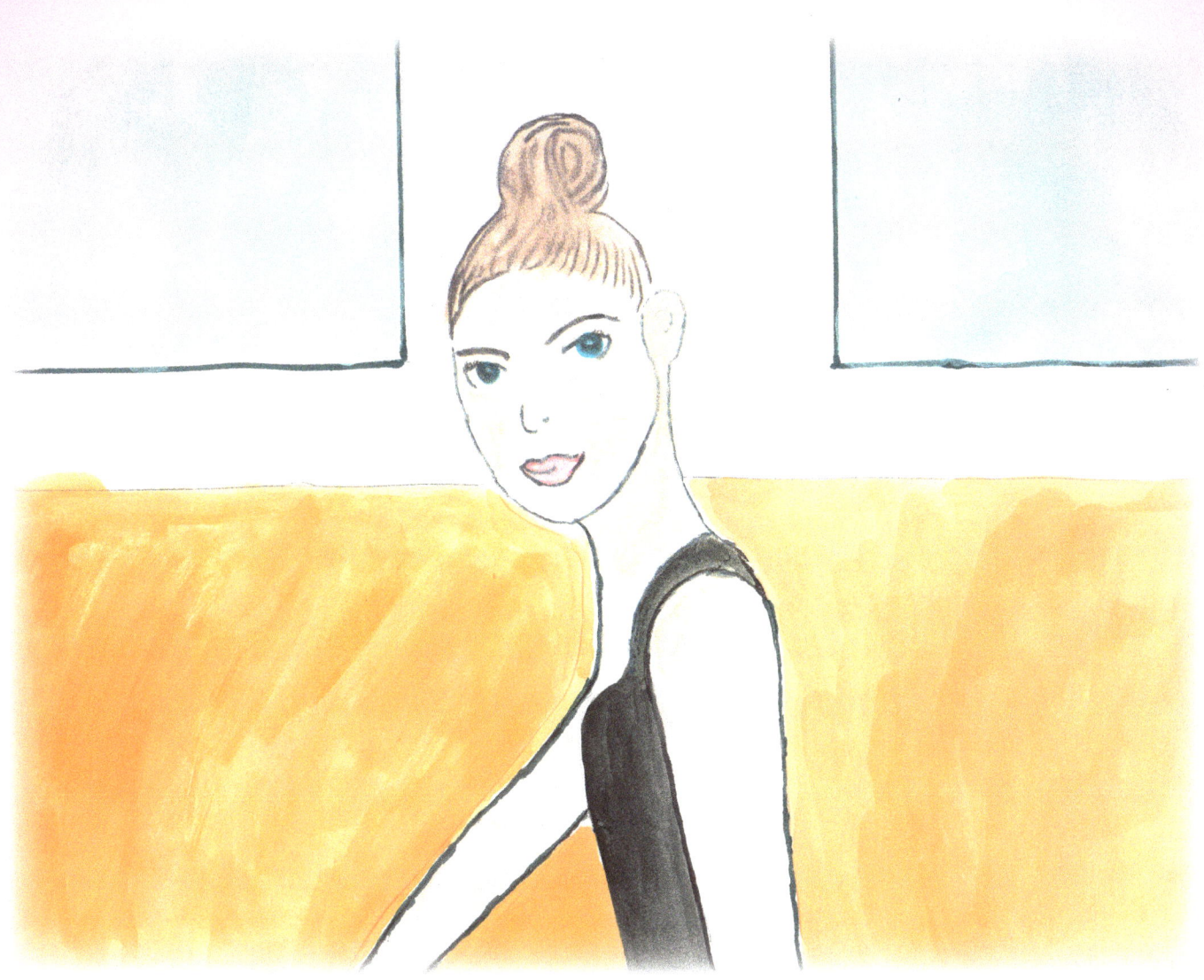

"We have a big surprise for everyone! We are adding a hip-hop dance to our recital. We have hired a professional choreographer and dancer from Los Angeles that will be coming in this weekend and putting a dance together for our recital." Ms. Anaïs yells, "Bring in your hip-hop shoes and get lots of rest for tomorrow!"

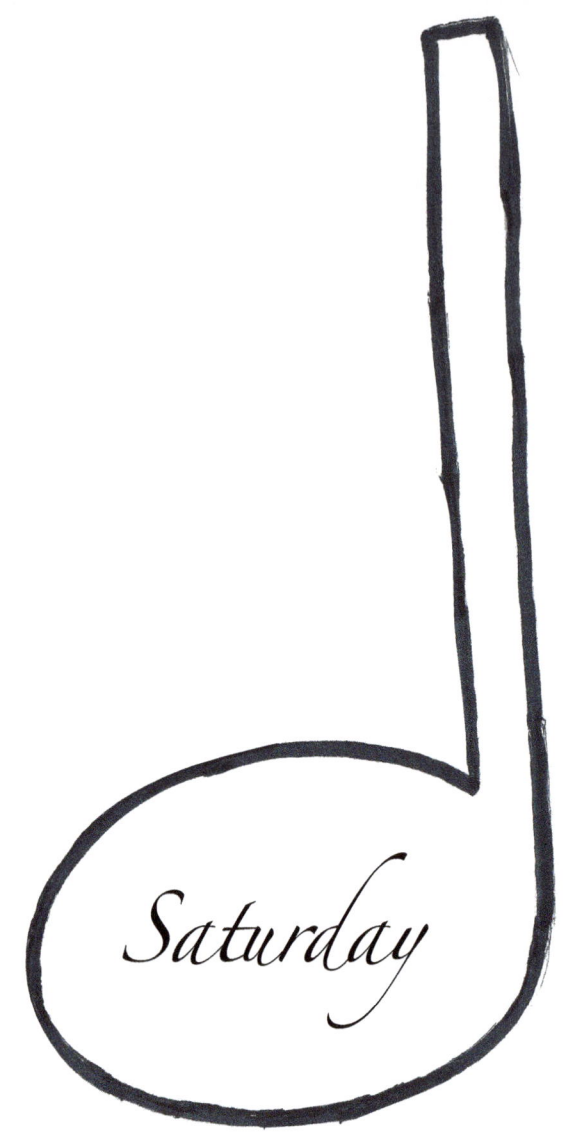

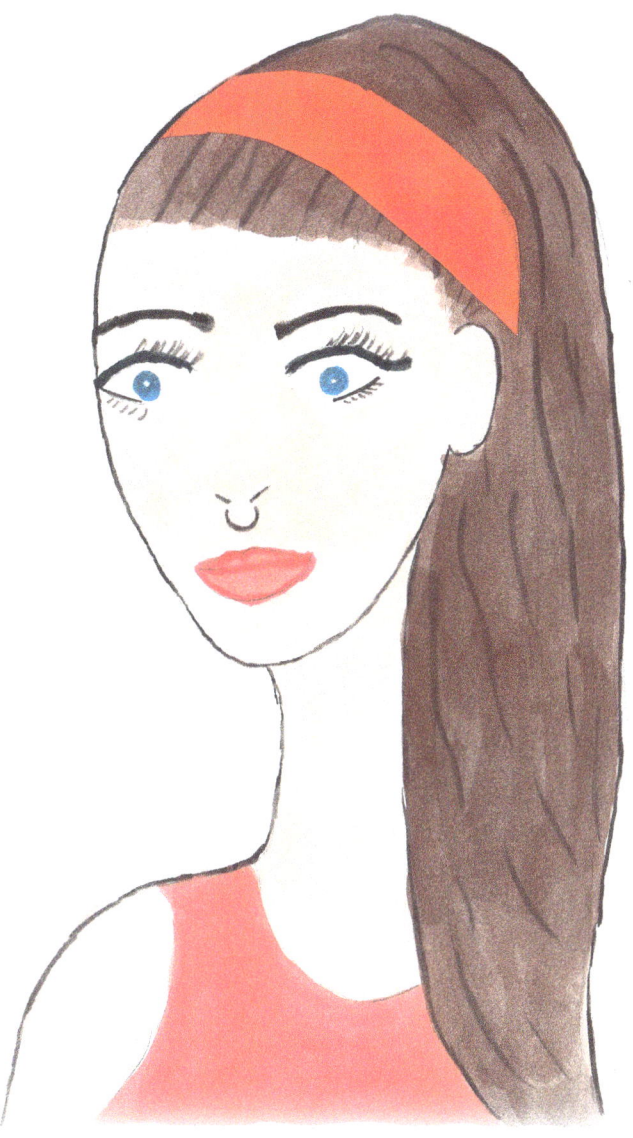

"Hey students! I would like to introduce our guest Missy, she has performed in many music videos, toured as a background dancer and choreographed for several pop singers. You are learning hip hop from the best." says Ms. Anaïs as she sits down getting ready to watch.

"Hi everyone!" Missy says happily, "today we are going to do a class and audition. I will be selecting 10 dancers end of class to do a hip-hop dance for your recital. I'm sorry there are only 10 openings for the routine. I don't want to think you are not a good dancer because you didn't get selected. It's all about being the best dancer you can be. We are all here to learn!"

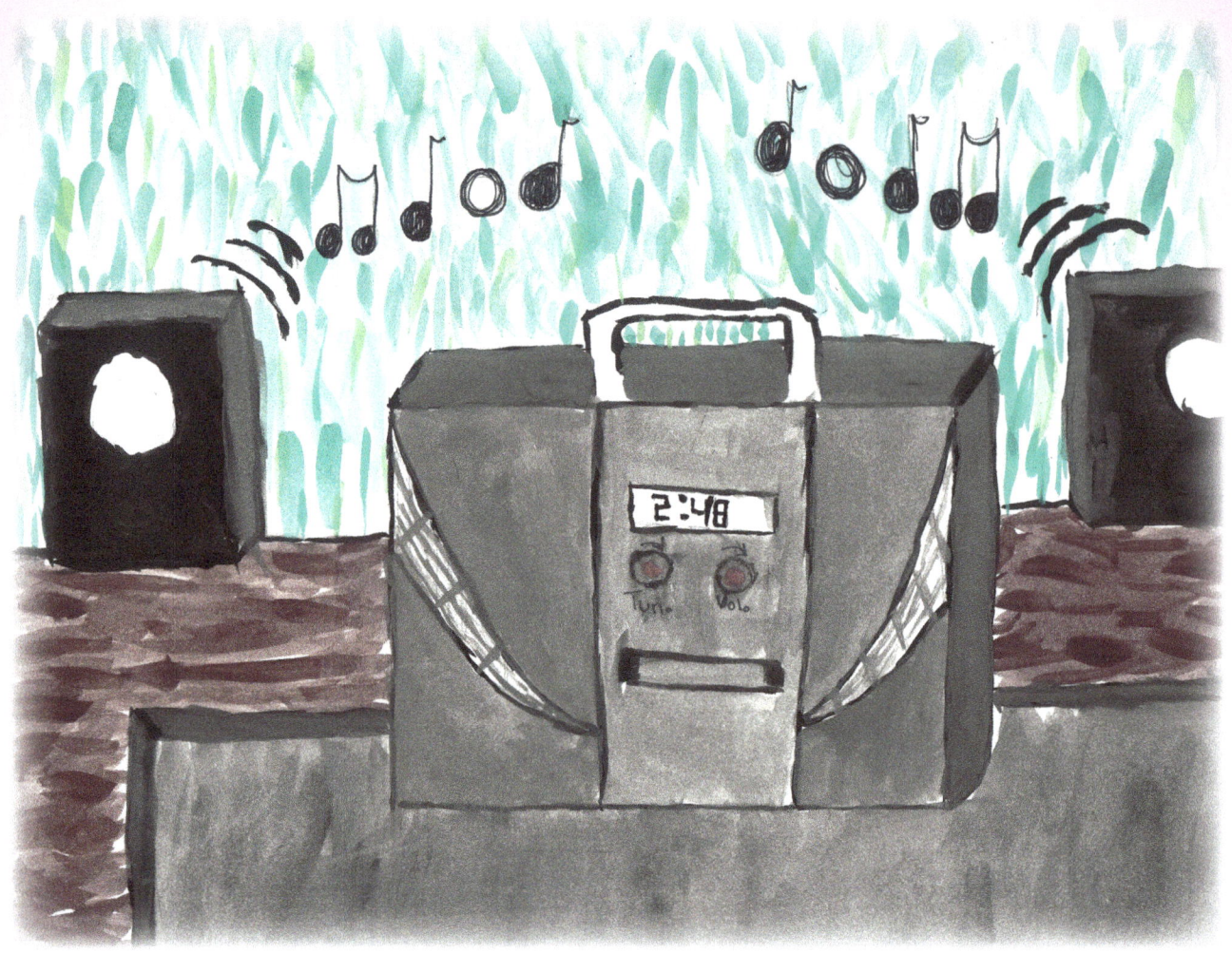

Music begins...

"Ready everyone? Let me do the dance first." says Missy. Missy does the dance and all the dancers are in awe of her. "Everybody ready. I'll do the steps slowly first. Step left, right, down turn and repeat. Turn. Step. Pose. Kick and finish! Repeat! Repeat!"

"We are going to separate and dance in groups" Missy says to the girls, as the music stops.

Music begins again...

1st group... 2nd group... 3rd group.

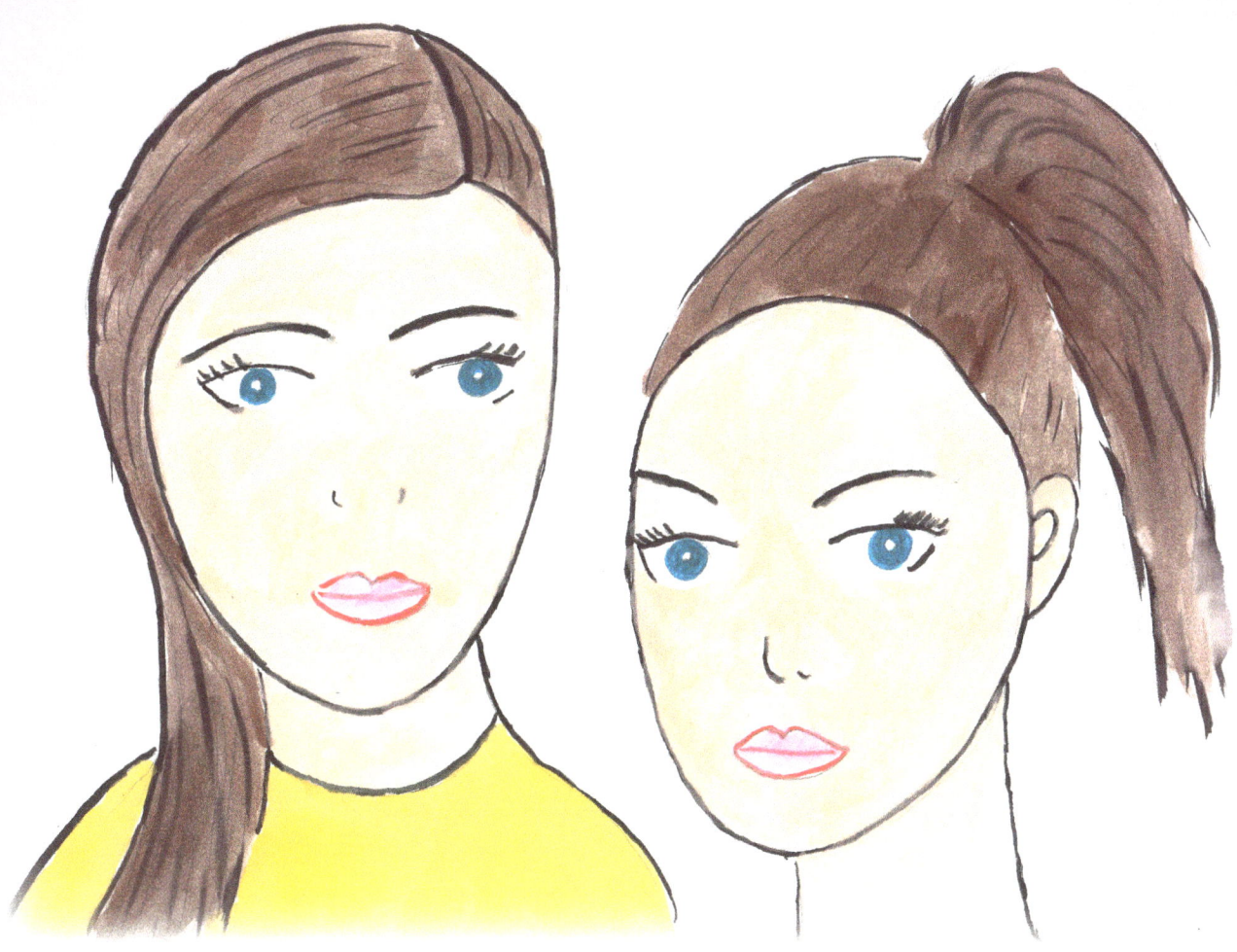

2 hours later....

Siena & Scarlett are exhausted.

   "This is harder than I thought!" complained Siena, "You are very good at this Scarlett, I cannot believe how fast you are picking it up. My feet are killing me."
   "The results will be posted tomorrow! Good luck girls!" announces Missy.

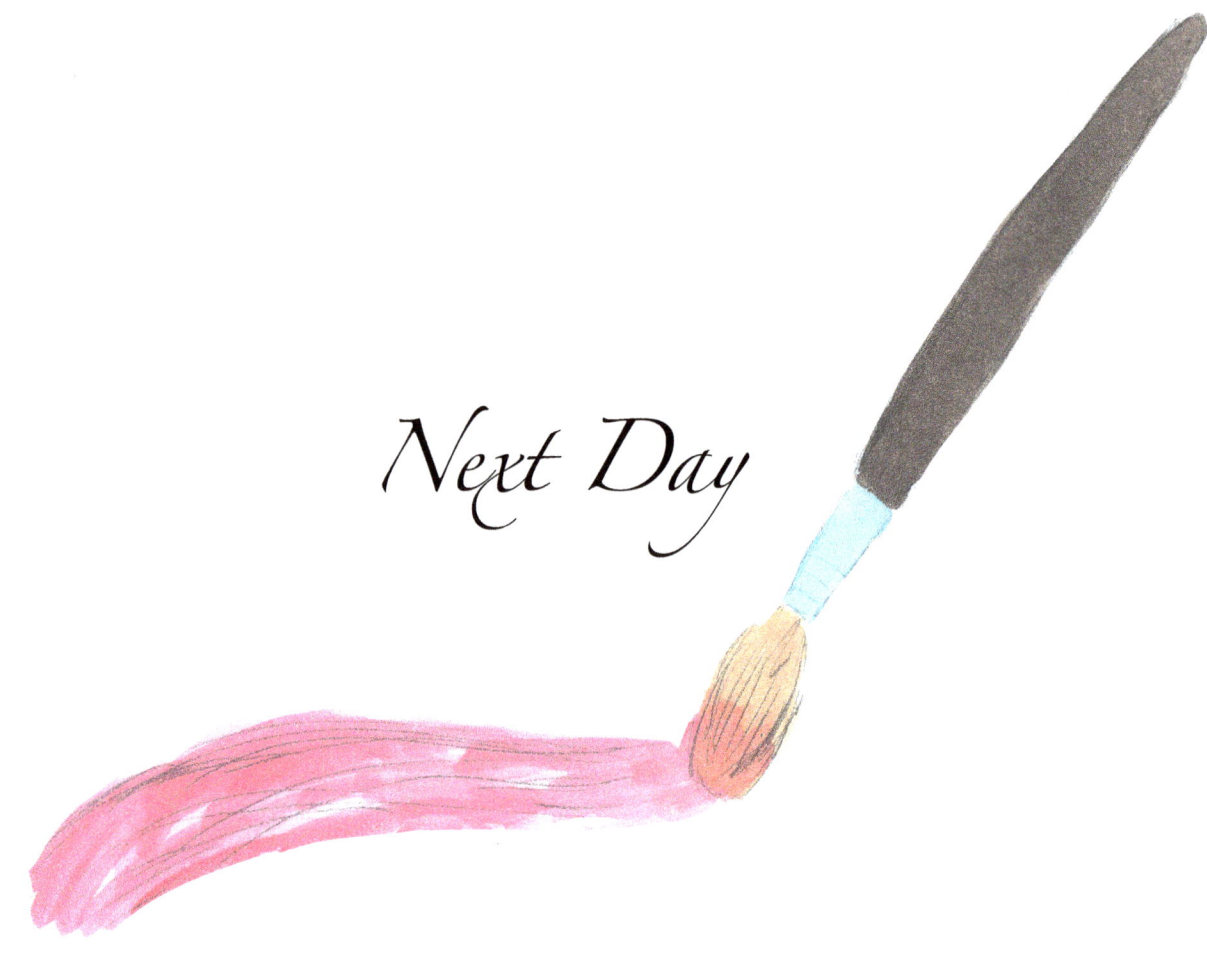

Next Day

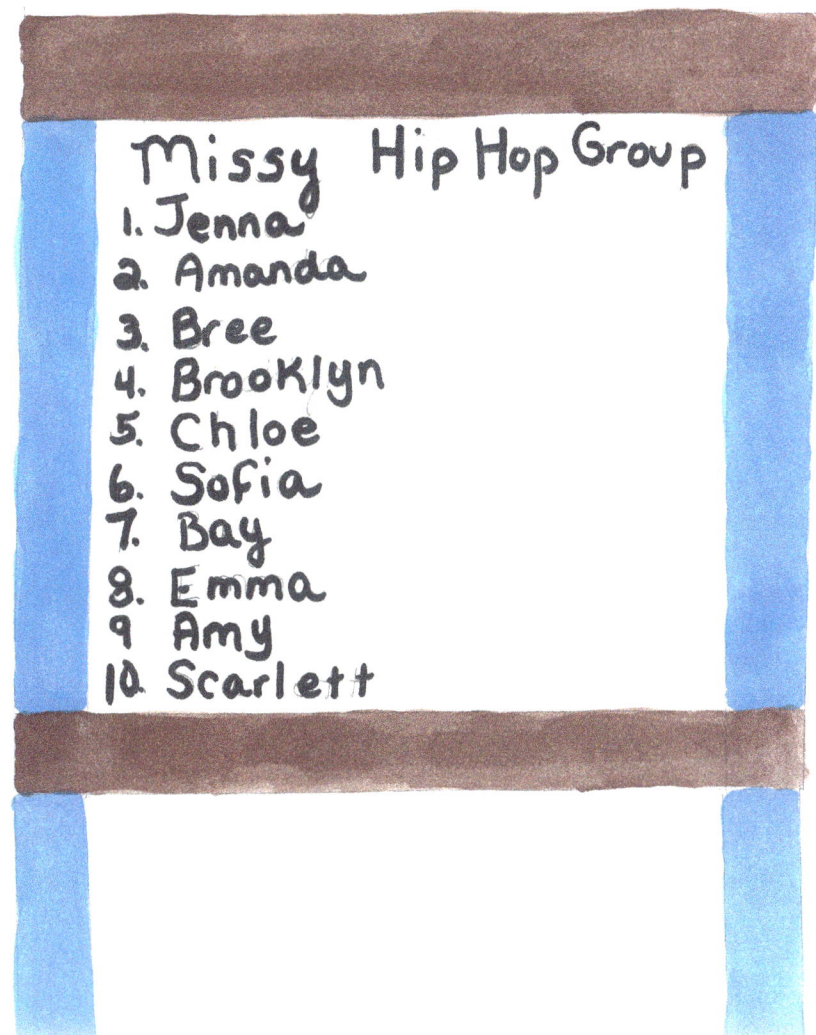

Missy Hip Hop Group
1. Jenna
2. Amanda
3. Bree
4. Brooklyn
5. Chloe
6. Sofia
7. Bay
8. Emma
9 Amy
10. Scarlett

"I got picked! I got picked!" says Scarlett, "Sorry you didn't get picked Siena."

"It's ok." says Siena, "You deserve it!"

"Everyone remember, tomorrow is dress rehearsal!" says Ms. Anaïs, "Our last rehearsal girls!"

Dress
Rehearsal

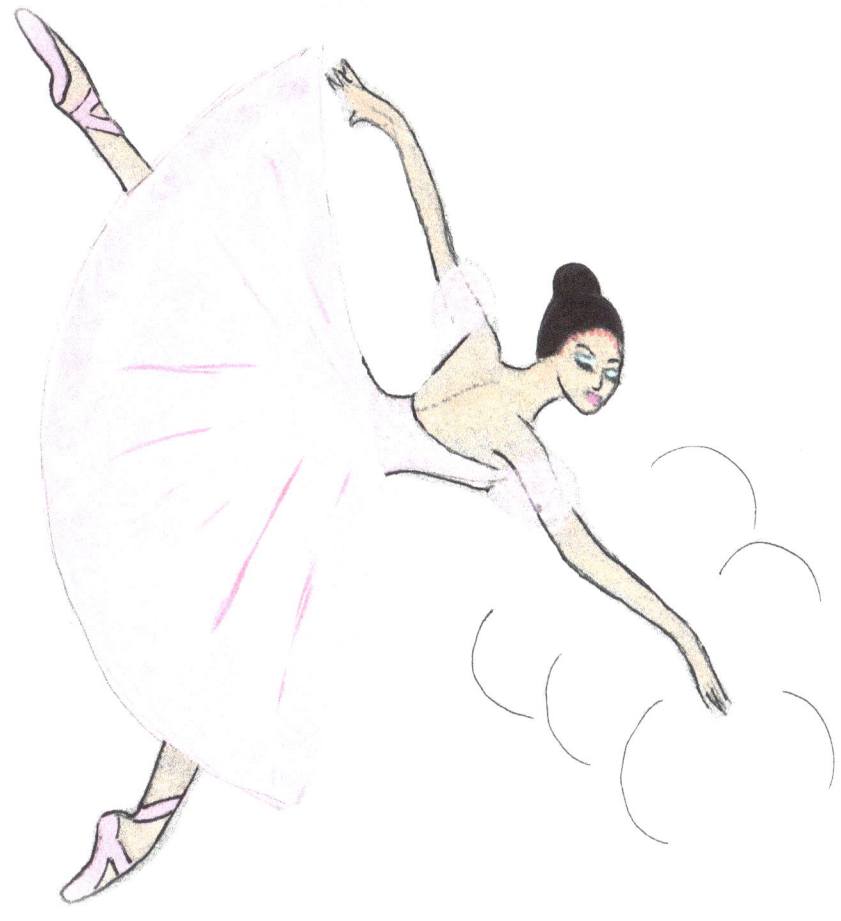

"Siena, Jennifer, Anna, Madeline, and Scarlett, we are ready for you. I want you to do your best. Le Petit Fleur is our best dance of the recital and it has to be great!" yells Ms. Anaïs, "Dancers, get in your beginning poses."

Music begins...

Jennifer, Anna, Madeline, & Scarlett chassé on stage and Siena enters gracefully.

"It's so beautiful" whispers are heard from the audience.

Siena gets ready for her grand jeté. All eyes are on her and all of sudden... Siena falls.

"OWWW!" yells Siena as she bursts into tears, "I can't move my leg!"

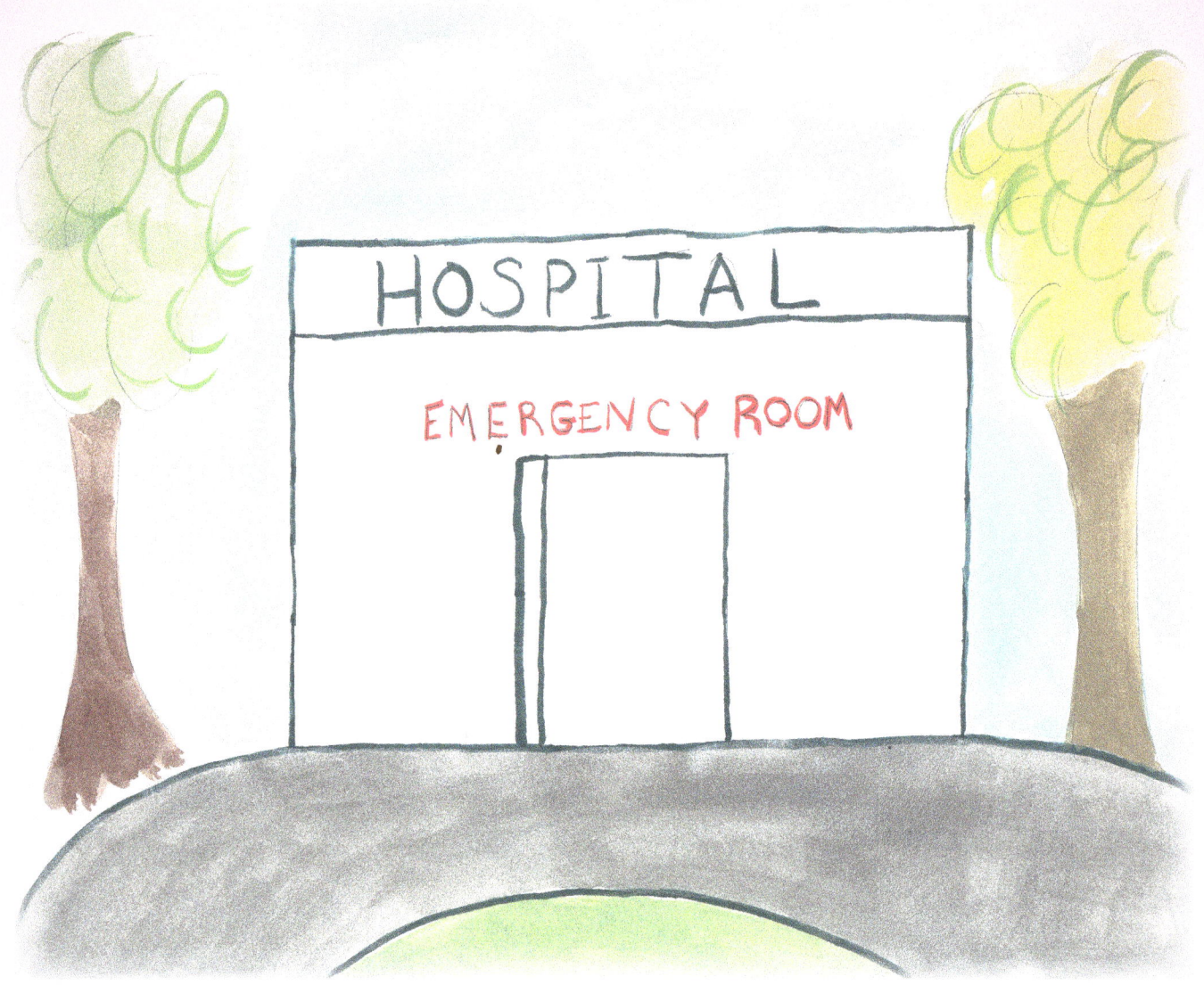

"I'm sorry Siena it's going to take a few months before you can dance." says the doctor, "It needs to heal. It's going to take time."

"What am I'm going to do? The recital is tomorrow..." says Siena tearing up, "Scarlett, you know the dance, I want you to step in my place," says Siena.

"I don't think I can do it, and plus, I know Ms. Anaïs will never agree to it!" says Scarlett.

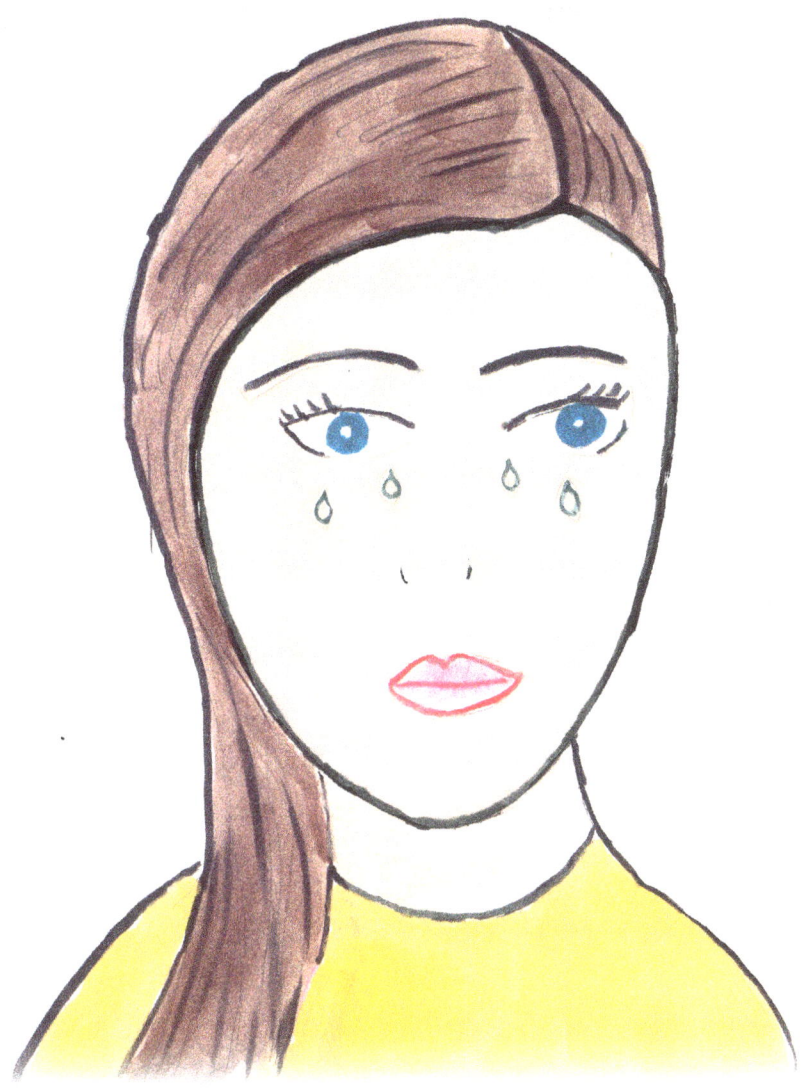

Ms. Anaïs walks in, "Siena, are you OK?"

"I'm sorry Ms. Anaïs, I will not be able to dance tomorrow, the doctor says I can not dance for a few months." says Siena, "Scarlett knows the dance, she rehearses with me. I know she can do it and she can fit in my costume perfectly."

"Hmmmm, I don't know. The role is a little advanced for her," says Ms. Anaïs, "Scarlett is the only one that really knows the dance," says Siena.

"Can you do it Scarlett?" says Ms. Anaïs.

Siena elbows Scarlett, "um...I... of course Ms. Anaïs." says Scarlett nervously and unsure about it.

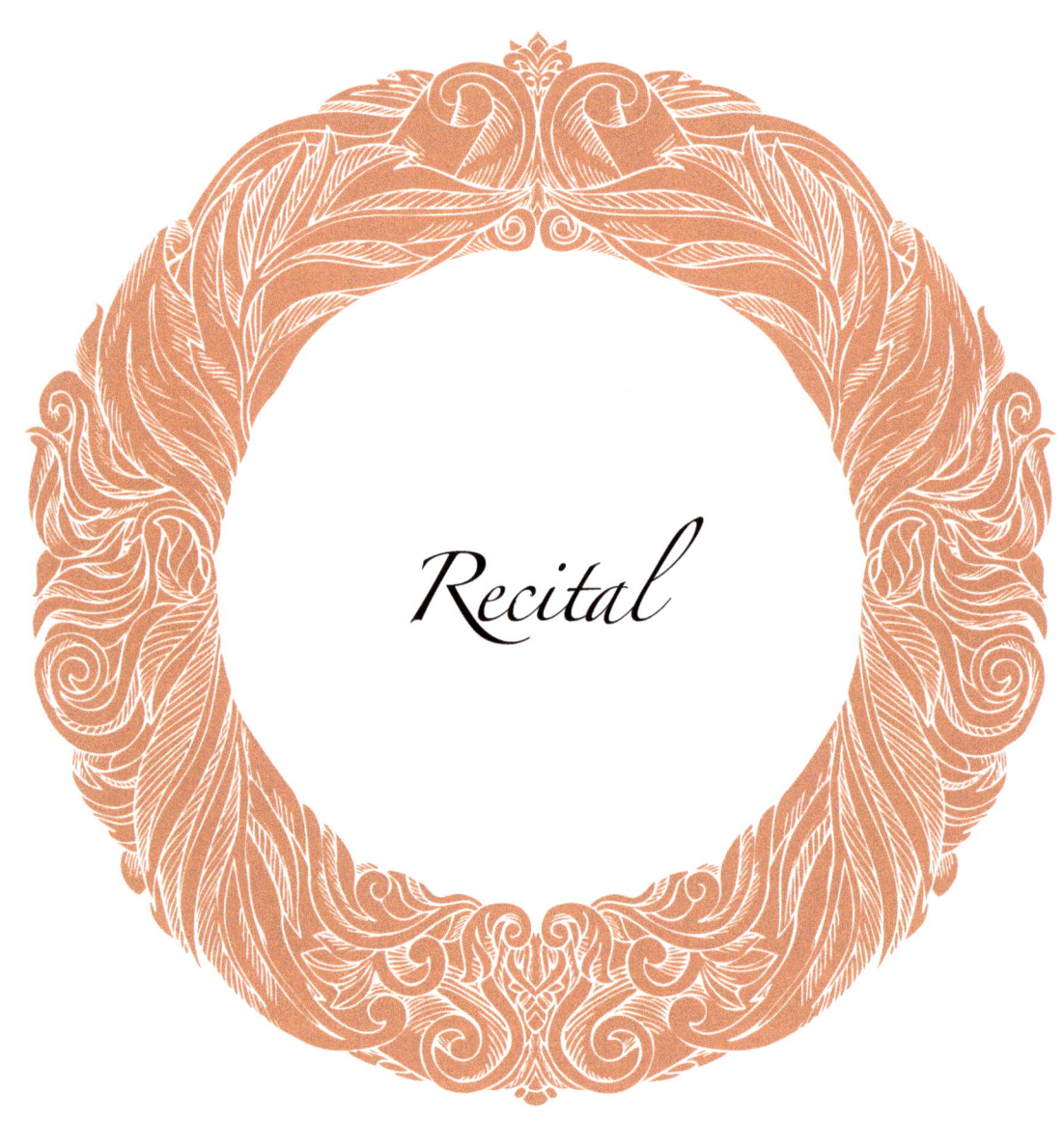

Recital

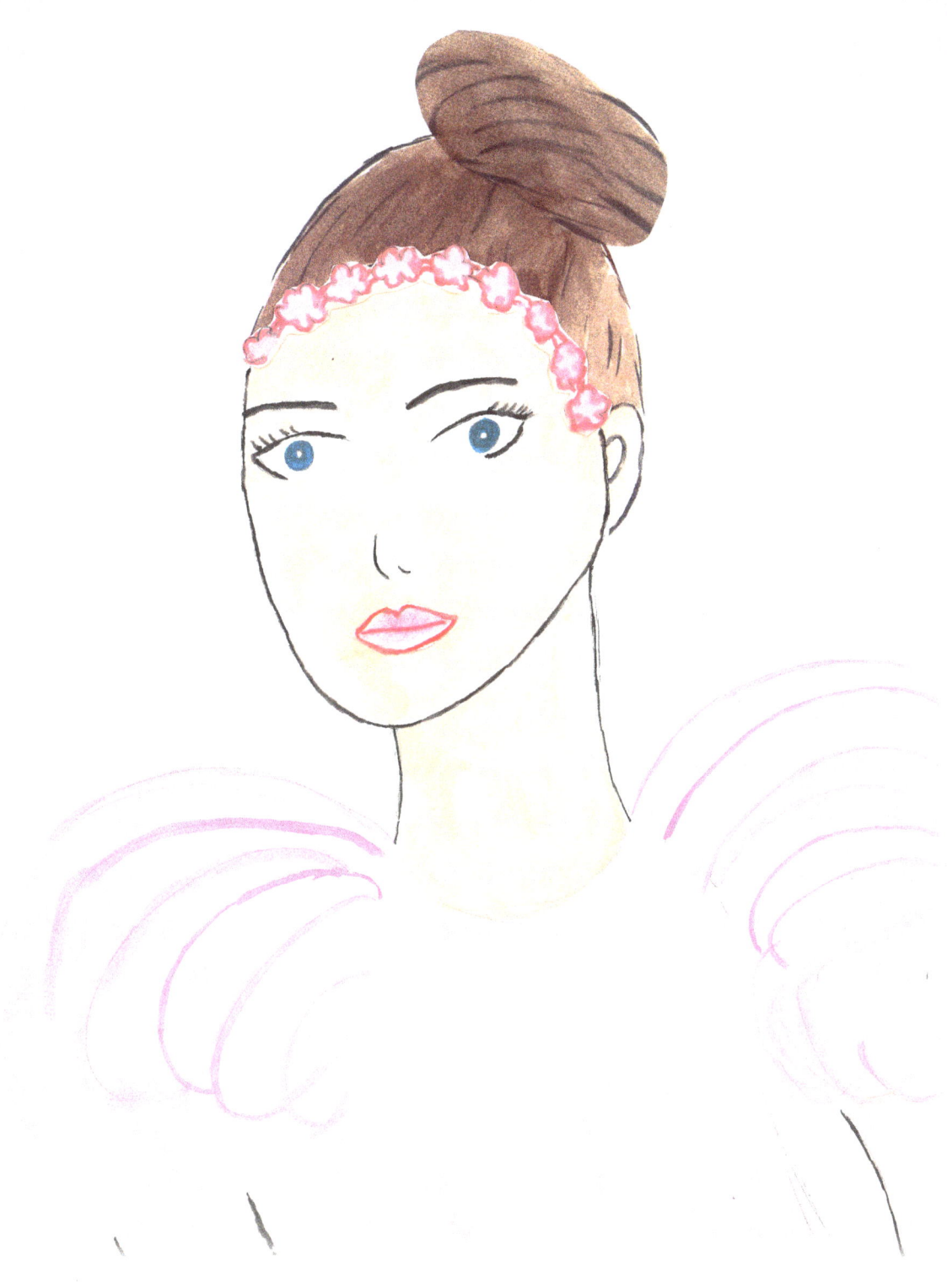

"I'm so nervous Siena, I don't think I can do it." says Scarlett.
   "This is your big chance to show Ms. Anaïs how talented you are. You look beautiful!" Siena replies, "You're the next number Scarlett."

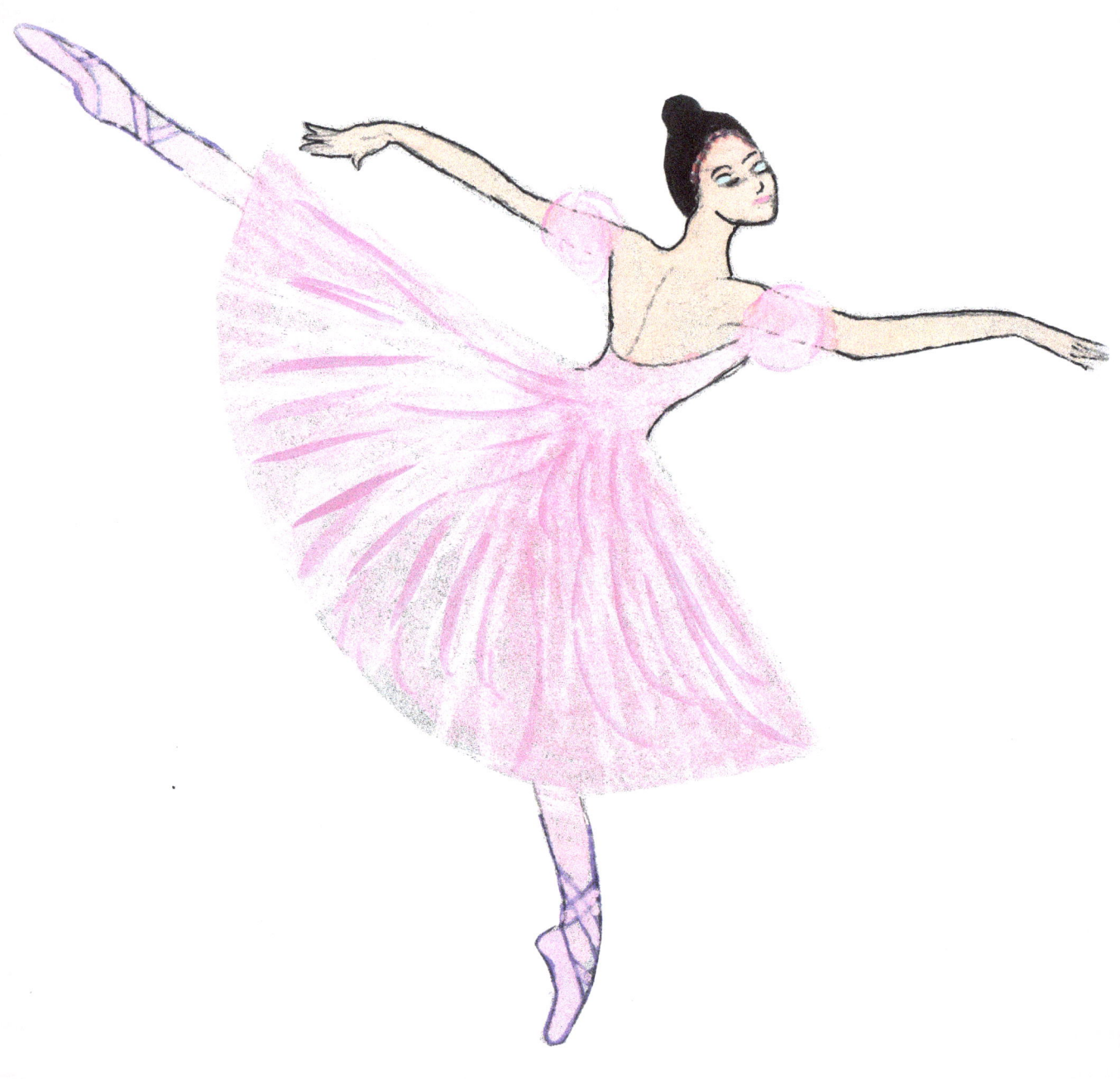

"Our next number is Le Petit Fleur. We had a last minute change with the main dancer. Her twin sister will be filling in for Siena. This dance is very special to me, and I hope you all enjoy it!" says Ms. Anaïs.

Scarlett waits anxiously off stage.

Music begins...

Scarlett watches the other dancers walk on stage in front of her. Scarlett makes her first step, she looks at the audience, and she tells herself I can do it! Scarlett begins to enjoy each step, feels the music with each step. She remembers Ms. Anaïs's advice that a dancer's role is to tell a story without any words. The room was quiet, Scarlett prepares for her leap. Scarlett nails it! The audience claps and yells. Scarlett walks off stage with the other dancers. Siena rushes to Scarlett and hugs her. "I knew you could do it!" says Siena.

"That was beautiful Scarlett. I think you are ready to step up more next year!" says Ms. Anaïs.

"All hip hop dancers, get ready you are up in 15 minutes!" yells one of the dance mothers.

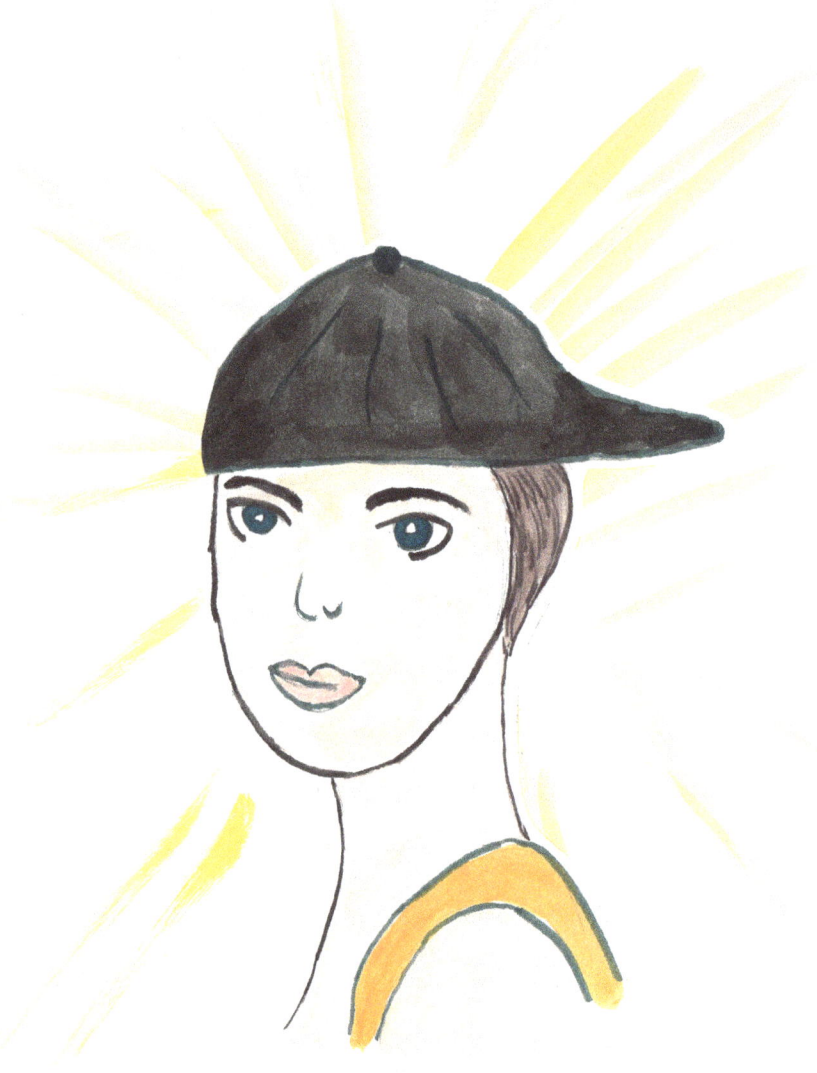

"This year we have something new for our recital and something new to me also. I'm classical trained in ballet and not too familiar with hip-hop. Ten of our girls got the opportunity to work with a professional choreographer from Los Angeles and perform in this dance!" says Ms. Anaïs.

Music begins....

The audience goes crazy. At the end the audience gives a standing ovation. The dancers go off stage to grab Ms. Anaïs to come on stage. They all dance on stage as the audience joins.

Evening After the Recital

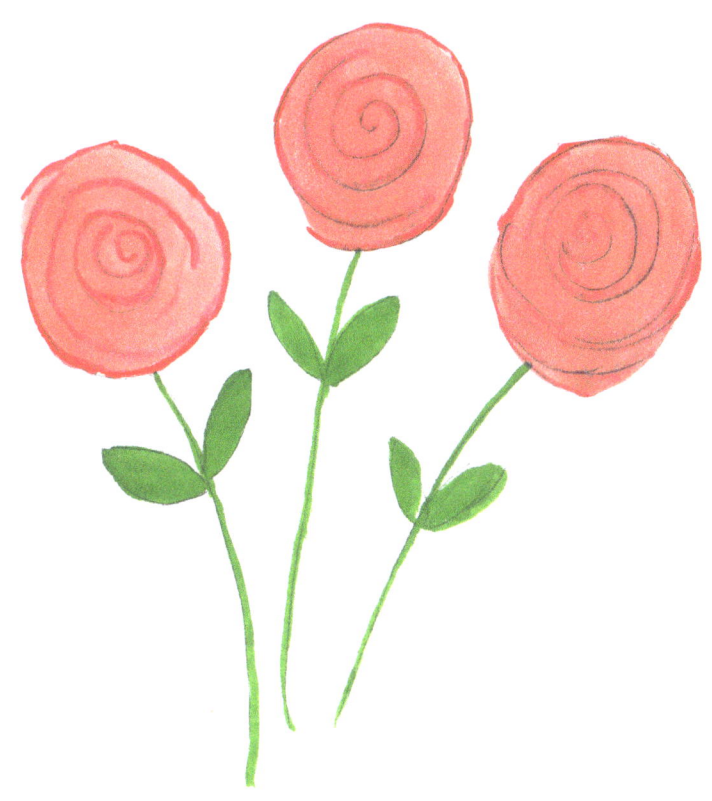

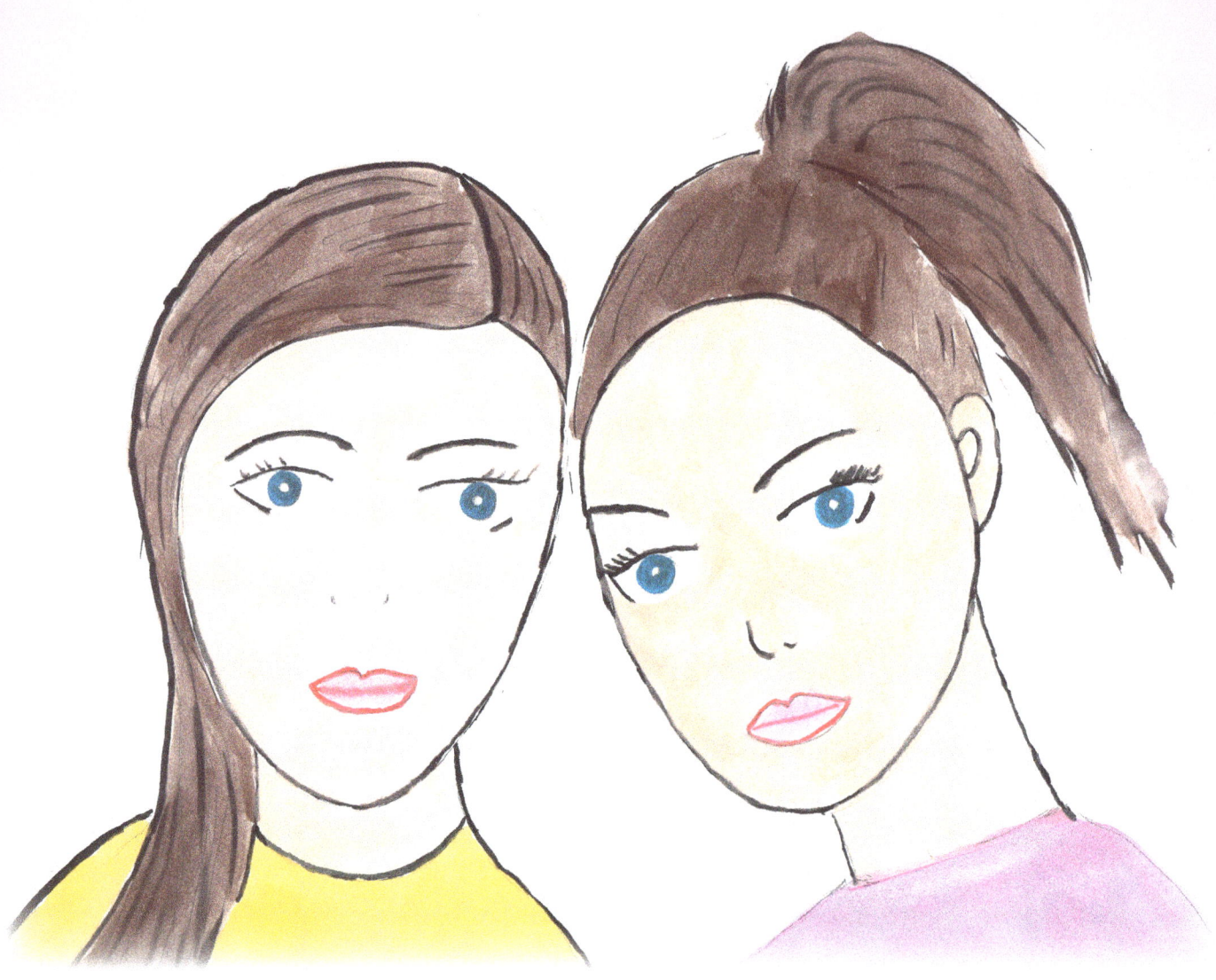

Scarlett thought to herself, "I cannot believe I did that, but I am so glad I tried."

The End

Ballet Terms

Dover Publications has graciously allowed the use of the terms below from the *Technical Manual and Dictionary of Classical Ballet.*

Plié
[*plee-AY*]
Bent, bending. A bending of the knee or knees. In all pliés the legs must be well turned out from the hips, the knees open and well over the toes, and the weight of the body evenly distributed on both feet, with the whole foot grasping the floor.

Chassé
[*sha-SAY*]
Chased. A step in which one foot literally chases the other foot out of its position; done in a series.

Battement
[*bat-MAHN*]
Beating. A beating action of the extended or bent leg.

Battement tendu [*bat-MAHN tahn-DEW*]: stretched

Battement frappé [*bat-MAHN fra-PAY*]: struck

Jeté, grand

[grahn zhuh-TAV]

Large <u>jeté</u>. In this step the legs are thrown to 90 degrees with a corresponding high jump.

Choreographer

This is the term applied to one who composes or invents ballets or dances.

www.ingramcontent.com/pod-product-compliance
Lightning Source LLC
Chambersburg PA
CBHW052143170526
45159CB00017B/3142